Managing Risk in the Construction Industry through Environmental Compliance:

On-Site BMP Checklists

I0470634

Jerome S. Arcaro

ISBN: 1490477500
ISBN-13: 978-1490477503

Jerome S. Arcaro

ABOUT THE AUTHOR

As a contractor, Jerome S. Arcaro served as an Environmental Compliance Project Manager for the US Navy for twenty-two years, starting with the Naval Facilities Engineering Command, Southern Division's (SOUTHDIV) Environmental Restoration Program Partnering initiative. Membership on the partnering teams included senior management and staff from the Navy, the US Environmental Protection Agency (EPA), various state Departments of Environmental Protection, contractors, and citizens.

Mr. Arcaro is also acknowledged for developing the Environmental Compliance Assessment, Training, and Tracking System (ECATTS®), a unique, cloud-based, job-specific environmental compliance training tool. This system is a risk-minimizing reference tool for contractors and is used to resolve job site environmental issues before violations occur. ECATTS has resulted in more than a 90 percent reduction of violations on military bases worldwide.

ACKNOWLEDGMENTS

The author would like to acknowledge the efforts of Mr. Barry Lester, who contributed to and helped with the editing of this book.

Barry Lester, PE, is a registered professional engineer with thirty years of experience in civil engineering, construction, and environmental compliance. Working for both government and the private sector, his projects have ranged from small commercial undertakings to multi-million dollar military construction projects. His roles have included certifying engineer for sewer and water supply systems, geotechnical evaluator, quality control engineer, and environmental compliance monitor. Mr. Lester served as a senior project manager under the Navy's Installation Restoration Program for environmental investigations at NAS Cecil Field, Florida.

DISCLAIMER

The Best Management Practices (BMPs) discussed in this guide are based on EPA regulations, guidelines, and rules for pollution prevention and environmental protection associated with construction. This guide provides an overview and does not include detailed discussion on each environmental regulation. The reader should refer to the US Environmental Protection Agency website (www.epa.gov) for more information and details on the regulations. Since states and local municipalities can enact their own rules for compliance (in support of or in addition to the EPA), it is important to seek out and understand these requirements before proceeding with construction activities.

This manual serves as a guide and reference based on the current primary laws and federal regulatory requirements and is not a compliance document to satisfy any regulations or permit stipulations. The reader is responsible for the review and implementation of federal, state, and local environmental regulations to determine how their project activity is governed by the specifics in those established laws. No warranty is expressed or implied. It is not a compliance document intended to satisfy any regulations or permit stipulations, nor is it a document to be submitted to any agency.

BMP checklists tailored to the construction process are appended to this manual. The checklists are not all-encompassing and may need to be modified to meet site-specific construction needs. These checklists are intended to assist in the identification of company approaches and to organize efforts in the best way possible. Readers should feel free to use these documents to develop more specific checklists for each construction activity.

MANAGING RISK THROUGH THE ADOPTION AND IMPLEMENTATION OF BMPS

It is important for every construction company to understand the implications of not following environmental rules and regulations. Disregarding environmental laws can open a company up to project delays, Notices of Violations (NOVs), fines, lawsuits, and much more. By integrating Best Management Practices (BMPs) into sound company Standard Operating Procedures (SOPs), a company can both manage risk and reduce costs.

This manual was designed to provide a better understanding of BMPs: what they are, how they can help, and how they should be used. Included in this manual are checklists, specific to construction-site projects, to better assist with on-the-job activities.

WHAT ARE BMPS?

BMPs can be described as practical and effective methods or techniques based on a range of experiences from the most successful businesses. BMPs provide a practical means of accomplishing an objective with the optimum use of resources. Organizations implement BMPs to reduce costs, avoid costly errors, operate more efficiently and effectively, and improve customer satisfaction. BMPs can be applied to every aspect of the construction process: planning, project design, permitting, site excavation, construction, and project closeout. The construction industry is also using BMPs to assess risk, select subcontractors and suppliers, and select sites.

Construction companies implement BMPs to ensure that project activities comply with federal, state, and local government environmental regulations, not only with the physical construction activities but also with policies and guidance from the boardroom to project close-out. BMPs continue to evolve, but they have proven successful when followed correctly.

HOW BMPS CAN HELP

BMPs are extremely important to a construction project but often overlooked. In cases of noncompliance, contractors are responsible for rectifying all problems caused by their employees or subcontractors. Research has shown that, unfortunately, many construction contractors have learned expensive lessons before implementing BMPs into their planning. This mistake can be due to lack of knowledge, reluctance to change, costs, or an attitude of "out of sight, out of mind," particularly if regulatory oversight is not expected.

Compliance monitoring is used by the EPA and other agencies to ensure that construction sites follow environmental laws and regulations at the federal, state, and local levels. This monitoring includes on-site visits by inspectors and the review of project permits, licenses, personnel, methods, and practices. If a deficiency is noted during this process, a NOV will be issued. Taking proactive measures, like implementing standard BMPs, can help avoid these NOVs.

Construction companies embracing BMPs typically achieve a higher level of customer satisfaction, keep safer sites, reduce environmental impacts, and make more profit than those companies that do not use BMPs.

Training is an important factor in facilitating BMPs and maintaining compliance. If a company's staff members are knowledgeable in the environmental laws and regulations specific to their jobs, they can perform their work in an environmentally safe manner, keeping the company free from NOVs and costly fines.

HOW TO UTILIZE BMPS

The BMPs discussed in this manual can be integrated by a company into its Standard Operating Procedures. In fact, introducing BMPs into SOPs will establish a solid foundation and guide all staff, subcontractors, and suppliers in understanding their environmental responsibilities and what is expected of them. Federal, state, and local environmental protection agencies have adopted stringent enforcement policies that require proper management of every project no matter the size. Building a solid foundation that includes training and the adoption of BMPs will ultimately lead to a higher level of overall compliance.

The use of BMPs for environmental compliance must be first integrated into the project during the design phase. From there, BMPs should continue to play a large role in every phase and in every activity performed. The checklists included are intended to provide a better understanding of which BMPs are needed for certain projects and assist with activity planning.

Jerome S. Arcaro

BMP CHECKLIST
Boardroom to Construction

The Code of Ethics and the foundation of guiding principals have to be united in the boardroom. They must be disseminated from the top down, throughout the entire organization, and to the worker hammering the very last nail.

BMPs for the Board:

- Establish written procedures for conducting business and monitoring compliance.
- Establish positions in management to carry out compliance activities.
- Keep abreast of the ever-changing regulatory environment through training and frequent monitoring of operations.
- Institute a culture that breaks down barriers between departments and staff members, and encourages involvement by all employees to be good environmental stewards (regardless of the position).
- Plan and budget for training, education, equipment, and other necessities to promote environmental compliance.
- Participate in the local community.
- Institute Best Management Practices as Standard Operating Procedures.
- Strive for continuous improvements.

Note: Contact your local or state environmental office for more information. Sources of BMP information include the state's environmental regulatory offices and state department of transportation offices.

BMP CHECKLIST
Effects of Environmental Legislation on the Construction Project

Vital to your success is the knowledge of environmental rules and regulations in your project community (which includes federal and state agencies and county, city, and municipal governments). Be clear on the laws and do your research prior to the start of your project.

BMPs for Following Environmental Laws:

- Seek out information from the local professional organizations in the state and city where the project is planned.
- Consult with local building officials; they may have a guidance document for use. (Larger municipalities have full-time planning and engineering staffs that can assist and provide information for your project.)
- Contact the state environmental agency about guidance documents and staff members who will assist with questions.
- Do your due diligence and investigate the construction site compliance needs, including:
  - Title search and deed restrictions, environmental leans and land use restrictions
  - Environmental Phase I ESA
  - Geotechnical and subsurface soil investigations
- Conduct recommended follow-up actions from the above investigations, if you wish to move forward with the project.
- Use competent environmental professionals to address identified areas of concern and to determine the specific needs of the project, the required approvals, licenses, fees, and regulatory rules that will apply to the construction effort.

Jerome S. Arcaro

Note: Contact your local or state environmental office for more information. Sources of BMP information include the state's environmental regulatory offices and state department of transportation offices.

BMP CHECKLIST
Project Team

Building a strong project team is the most critical step in completing a successful construction project. Project teams are comprised of many stakeholders: owner, architect, engineer, general contractor, site supervisors, subcontractors, suppliers, the EPA, and state, county, and city governments, among others. Each project will have its own dynamics and personality makeups; however, implementing BMPs will enhance team performance and productivity. Use partnering for positive team building and promoting cooperation among all stakeholders.

Once the owner selects an architect, engineer, and general contractor, he or she must finalize any contractual or budgetary issues and prepare a Project Control Plan (sometimes called a Project Operations and Control Plan or Project Communications Plan).

BMPs for Preparing a Project Control Plan:

- Build an organizational chart.
- Decide team member positions and responsibilities.
- Share contact information.
- Finalize communications control for formal agency inquiries.
- Appoint the primary Point of Contact for site inspections and regulatory inquiries, and name an authorized backup.
- Build a site map.
- Decide on emergency evacuation procedures.
- List locations, routes, and phone numbers of hospitals, police, and fire stations.

- List phone numbers for local environmental departments and other agencies assigned to the project.

Note: Contact your local or state environmental office for more information. Sources of BMP information include the state's environmental regulatory offices and state department of transportation offices.

BMP CHECKLIST
Preparing for an Environmental Inspection

If your construction site is visited by an environmental agency for an inspection, your worksite environmental controls and pollution prevention procedures need to be in place. A preemptive technique to plan for inspections—and instruct employees and supervisors on how to act and respond—will be to conduct self-inspections. The self-inspections should focus on compliance with the approved design plans, SWPPP, permits, and other conditions or stipulations placed on the project by governing authorities.

Official site inspections will generally involve four actions:

1. Introduction by official(s) and an opening meeting
2. Construction site walk-through
3. Closing meeting
4. An agency letter (Any findings and/or violations will be mailed to the construction company.)

BMPs for Preparing for an Environmental Inspection:

- Monitor all activities.
- Communicate with all workers about the importance of environmental awareness and worksite safety.
- Make sure training is up to date and current certificates of completion are on file when training is required for workers.
- Review work procedures to ensure they are up to date with the most current regulations.
- Make sure all environmental records are up to date, easily accessible, and ready for review.

- Clearly post building permits, environmental permits, and other official notices required by law.
- Identify hazardous materials/hazardous waste on-site and ensure proper storage and spill containment.
- Maintain Material Safety Data Sheets (MSDS) for all substances and materials brought onto the worksite.
- Ensure all signage and placards are intact and legible.
- Double check container integrity and spill containment measures if petroleum storage tanks, chemical tanks or fifty-five gallon drums of substances are on-site.
- Conduct routine housekeeping and maintain a clean, organized job site.
- Do not let trash or waste piles build up and always have proper dumpsters or containers available.
- Make sure access control measures, including fences, gates, locks and walkways, are in place.
- Implement security measures, as necessary.
- Route truck and construction traffic through site in a safe manner with necessary signage and signal controls.
- Appoint a person to serve as the Point of Contact for the inspection. (This person can be the site supervisor, environmental manager or someone familiar with the site design and environmental controls and has regulatory knowledge of permits, licenses, and applicable laws, rules and regulations. Also, assign a back-up in case the primary person is unavailable.)
- Accompany the inspector at all times while on the job site.
- Ask the inspector the reason for inspection. (It could be the result of a complaint, a routine inspection, or a special compliance effort.)
- Be cooperative during the inspection process and ask for a follow-up letter or inspection report.

- Conduct a mock inspection. Discuss openly with participants the manner in which it played out, and identify opportunities for improvement.

Note: Contact your local or state environmental office for more information. Sources of BMP information include the state's environmental regulatory offices and state department of transportation offices.

BMP CHECKLIST
Response to a Notice of Violation

The Notice of Violation letter is not the end of the enforcement action but the beginning. Agencies gather information to pursue further actions and possible fines and penalties. Preparation of the BMPs for response to a NOV situation should include the following, plus other means or methods deemed necessary for the specific infractions to be remedied.

BMPs for Responding to a NOV:

- Carefully read the "Notice of Violation" and commit to understanding all of the items identified.
- Seek out answers to questions you do not understand.
- Meet with staff, workers, and management (include attorney, if necessary) to jointly review the NOV.
- Contact the agency by phone or email or have the company attorney do so.
- Keep thorough records and documentation during the NOV period.
- Make every effort to correct deficiencies and comply with the NOV orders.
- Answer each violation separately when writing official letters of correspondence.
- Make sure to reference the license number, facility number, or other official registrant number listed on the NOV, along with any compliance number received.
- Inform the agency of steps taken to correct each violation and how the company will prevent recurrence.
- Record and document the date that compliance was achieved.

- Take photographs of the corrective measures once in place and have them available for the inspector or agency representative.
- Do not request a change to your license or permit when answering a NOV because doing so will delay processing your response and may raise additional questions from the agency.

Note: Contact your local or state environmental office for more information. Sources of BMP information include the state's environmental regulatory offices and state department of transportation offices.

BMP CHECKLIST
Construction Site Controls: Spill Prevention and Control

All construction sites where chemicals or hazardous materials are used and stored require the use of BMPs for spill prevention and quick response to reduce the potential for polluting storm drains and water bodies with released contaminants. The chemicals and hazardous wastes commonly found at a construction site include soil stabilizers and binders, dust palliatives, herbicides, growth inhibitors, fertilizers, fuels, lubricants, paints, and solvents.

BMPs for Spills:

Be prepared for spills.
* Locate and label spill kits nearby for quick access.
* Keep records of chemicals and maintain all Material Safety Data Sheets (MSDS).
* Keep spill kits filled with the following items:
  * A container to hold spill clean-up debris such as a five-gallon bucket with a sealable lid or thick contractor-grade plastic bags
  * Spare fifty-five-gallon drums and eighty-five gallon over-pack drums on-site for use with larger spills
  * Granular absorbent, absorbent pads and boom
  * Dust pan and broom for sweeping up granular absorbent (If cleaning flammable materials, use a dust pan that is a spark-free tool.)
  * A pump to empty leaking drums, plugs, and patching materials for drums, if it is a larger spill
  * Labels and hazardous waste stickers to properly mark containers of spill cleanup debris (Make sure contents,

time and date, and contact information are on the labels.)
- Forceps, tongs, or other tools to pick up contaminated debris or broken glass
- Basic First Aid Kit
- Additional specific first aid materials such as:
  - Hydrofluoric Acid: Calcium gluconate gel (2.5%) for skin contact
  - Chloroform/Phenol: Isopropanol, polyethylene glycol 300 or polyethylene glycol 400 for skin contact

Respond to spills.
- Make sure spill responders are trained and license certified (if necessary to satisfy applicable state and federal regulations).
- Have training to include BMPs for spill response actions.
- Incorporate spill response topics and information into daily safety meetings.
- Contain the spill.
- Recover the spilled material.
- Clean the spill area.
- Use absorbent materials.
- Do not hose down the area.
- Dispose of cleanup materials appropriately.
- Surround the spill with absorbent materials to contain the spill on impermeable surfaces such as pavement and concrete.
- Construct an earthen dike to contain the spill on dirt areas.
- Dig up contaminated soil and dispose of it properly off-site after obtaining permits and approvals as needed.
- Cover the spill with plastic, a tarp, or other means to prevent co-mingling of the water and the spilled material and to

prevent the spill from contaminating runoff and leaving the construction site, if the spill occurs during a rain event.

- Call 911 or another emergency number for fire and police, if needed. (Fire fighters are trained in response procedures.)
- Notify the National Response Center at 800-424-8802 if a spill occurs and the volume of the spill meets or exceeds the quantities established by the federal government. Follow up with a written report.
- Employ a spill response contractor or hazardous material team if the spill is of a size that cannot be contained with the contractor's workforce, or if there are not sufficiently trained employees to conduct the work. (The response to highly toxic material spills or strictly regulated materials must always include properly trained and certified hazardous material responders.)

Note: Contact your local or state environmental office for more information. Sources of BMP information include the state's environmental regulatory offices and state department of transportation offices.

BMP CHECKLIST
Construction Site Controls: Waste Management

Materials used for construction activities should be delivered
and stored using methods that prevent the pollution of receiving
waters. Some of the more common pollutants include petroleum
products, pesticides, herbicides, fertilizers, detergents, plasters,
acids, lime, glues, adhesives, paints, and solvents.

BMPs for Waste Management:

- Store materials indoors in existing structures when available.
- Meet building and fire code requirements for temporary
  storage sheds.
- Locate materials away from vehicle traffic.
- Post storage instructions.
- Train employees in proper storage and handling procedures.
- Do not store hazardous materials directly on the ground.
- Store liquid chemicals in drums, bags on pallets and under
  cover, and in a secondary container.
- Store materials in original containers with their original
  product labels.
- Keep Material Safety Data Sheets (MSDS) for all materials
  stored on-site.
- Do not store incompatible materials in the same storage shed
  or area.
- Keep enough space between stored containers to allow
  cleanup of spills and emergency response.
- Maintain secondary containment for storage that is capable
  of containing sufficient volume for rainfall from a twenty-
  four hour, twenty-five year storm event, plus the greater
  volume from 10 percent of the aggregate amount of mate-

rial from all containers, or 100 percent of the capacity of the largest container within its perimeter, whichever is greater.

- Remove accumulated rainwater or spills from containment areas as soon as possible.
- Store those materials delivered in bags and boxes on pallets.
- Cover bagged and boxed materials prior to rain events to protect materials from wind and precipitation. (Do this on non-working days.)
- Contain and clean up spills immediately in accordance with BMPs for Spill Prevention and Control.

Note: Contact your local or state environmental office for more information. Sources of BMP information include the state's environmental regulatory offices and state department of transportation offices.

BMP CHECKLIST
Construction Site Controls: Erosion Prevention

Preventive measures should be used for erosion control during and after site preparation to ensure sediment retention and stabilization. Erosion can be caused by rainfall, flowing water, and even wind.

BMPs for Erosion Prevention:

- Phasing and Construction Sequencing
- Surface Roughening
- Mulching
- Erosion Control Blankets (ECB)
- Turf Reinforcement Mats (TRMs)
- Flexible Growth Matrix (FGM)
- Bonded Fiber Matrix (BFM)
- Sodding Riprap
- Outlet Protection
- Dust Control
- Polyacrylamide (PAM)
- Permanent Seeding
- Reinforcement Matting
- Temporary and Permanent Seeding

Other important measures include the following:

- Keep cut and fill slopes no steeper than 3H:1V unless special provisions are made.
- Do not place cuts or fills close to property lines or near other properties without special provisions.

- Use subsurface drains to intercept seepage flow and maintain slope stability.
- Do not place fill near property lines where it can wash onto other property.
- Keep fill away from channel banks to prevent sediment disposition into water streams and possible bank failure.
- Indicate all borrow areas and disposal areas on the project plans.
- Provide adequate floodways (away from the construction site) to a proper water outlet if necessary to prevent significant erosion and off-site flooding.

Note: Contact your local or state environmental office for more information. Sources of BMP information include the state's environmental regulatory offices and state department of transportation offices.

BMP CHECKLIST
Construction Site Controls: Dust Control

Dust control measures are necessary to control wind erosion, especially when surface soil is loose or dry and vegetation is limited or absent. When the wind is strong and construction vehicles disturb the soil, the wind erodes and transports sediment off-site in the form of fugitive dust. This dust can be washed into receiving bodies of water by the next rainfall. Fugitive dust is not only a nuisance for neighbors, it settles on automobiles, structures and windows, and enters nearby homes. As a consequence, people with respiratory problems can experience breathing difficulties. In addition, gusts of dusty wind can become a safety concern since it can blind motorists, equipment operators, and laborers.

BMPs for Dust Control:

- Utilize dust control methods whenever there are off-site impacts.
- Use dust control on all exposed soil that is subject to wind erosion.
- Use dust control during periods of drought.
- Implement dust control until final stabilization is reached.
- Add additional dust control or re-spray area as necessary to keep dust to a minimum.
- Spray exposed soil areas with water only or approved dust control agents.
- Apply dust control in accordance with manufacturer's standard practices.
- Exercise care when applying water or dust palliative to

prevent the washing of sediment off-site, into storm drains or receiving waters.

- Do not apply too much so that runoff occurs.
- Cover small stockpiles as an alternative to applying water or dust palliative.
- Apply vegetative covers to help reduce wind erosion.
- Use mulch as a temporary measure to stabilize soil.
- Use sprinkling to control suspension of particles and help dust settle out of the air.
- Use Calcium Chloride to help keep soil moist (but not in heavy amounts that could lead to a pollutant problem).
- Use spray-applied adhesives on mineral soils to prevent them from blowing away.
- Use barrier fences to block wind near ground level.

Note: Contact your local or state environmental office for more information. Sources of BMP information include the state's environmental regulatory offices and state department of transportation offices.

BMP CHECKLIST
Construction Site Controls: Protection of Trees

Trees provide erosion and sediment control, protect the watershed, control dust, reduce noise, and provide shade.

BMPs for Protecting Trees:

- Plan properly to get the easiest and most economical way to ensure tree preservation.
- Select trees for retention then accurately mark them on building plans, as well as in the field, prior to any work performed.
- Discuss tree preservation with all stakeholders.
- Place the limits of clearing around trees outside the drip line (directly under the edges of the outermost branches).
- Keep heavy equipment and vehicular traffic (and stockpiles) away from trees.
- Do not use fires within 100 feet of drip lines.
- Do not store toxic chemicals or waste within 100 feet of drip lines.
- Do not perform trenching inside of crown spreads and avoid damaging large tree roots.
- Use tunneling in lieu of trenching to preserve the tree's root system.

Note: Contact your local or state environmental office for more information. Sources of BMP information include the state's environmental regulatory offices and state department of transportation offices.

BMP CHECKLIST
Construction Site Controls: Litter Control

Implementing litter control methods can both prevent litter from becoming pollution and improve the aesthetics of the area. Sources of easily controlled litter include lawn clippings, pet waste, trash, oil, and chemicals. Litter can also decay and thereby create a high oxygen demand in the water.

BMPs for Litter Control:

- Participating personally is critical to effectively promoting litter control.
- Keeping street gutters free of leaves and lawn clippings can substantially reduce phosphorous levels in affected surface waters.
- Eliminating pet waste will eliminate a major source of bacteria in storm water runoff.
- Placing litter containers in convenient locations and frequently disposing the litter off-site will help to prevent overflow.
- Promoting recycling programs and developing worker education programs should be a priority.

Note: Contact your local or state environmental office for more information. Sources of BMP information include the state's environmental regulatory offices and state department of transportation offices.

BMP CHECKLIST
Construction Site Controls: Vehicle and Equipment Washing

Vehicle and equipment washing should be accomplished off-site to keep contaminants out of the construction area, adjacent receiving waters, and storm drains. Rinse water from such cleaning contains wastes such as sediment, petroleum, lubricants, residues, soaps, and solvents. If washing is to be conducted on-site, follow the relevant BMPs.

BMPs for Vehicle and Equipment Washing:

- Contain and dispose of all waste from on-site cleaning operations at an off-site permitted disposal facility.
- Post a sign identifying the vehicle and equipment wash.
- Locate the wash area away from storm drain inlets, drainage facilities, and watercourses.
- Create a berm to contain runoff and prevent run-on.
- Use a sump pump for the collection and disposal of wash water.

Note: Contact your local or state environmental office for more information. Sources of BMP information include the state's environmental regulatory offices and state department of transportation offices.

BMP CHECKLIST
Construction Site Controls: Runoff Control and Conveyance

The amount of sediment released from storm water runoff at construction sites is a water quality issue, particularly for small streams. Polluted runoff at construction sites with no controls is significantly greater than that from sites with controls. During storms, sediment-laden runoff can overcome a small stream channel's capacity and cause scouring, erosion, and destruction of vegetative cover.

BMPs for Runoff Control and Conveyance:

- Utilize the following:
    - Pipe Slope Drains
    - Temporary Stream Crossing
    - Diversion Measures
    - Level Spreader
    - Subsurface Drains
    - Construction De-watering

Note: Contact your local or state environmental office for more information. Sources of BMP information include the state's environmental regulatory offices and state department of transportation offices.

BMP CHECKLIST
Construction Site Controls: Sediment Control

The results of uncontrolled runoff at construction sites are a great concern for water quality. The impact from sediment transport to streams and water bodies can be threatening to habitats for fish and aquatic life through pollutants such as pesticides, petroleum, chemicals, solvents, asphalt, acids, and other substances.

BMPs for Sediment Control:

- Utilize the following:
  - Stabilized Construction Entrance
  - Temporary Sediment Basin
  - Temporary Sediment Trap
  - Silt Fence
  - Rock Check Dams
  - Sediment Tubes
  - Storm Drain Inlet Protection
  - Rock Dikes

Note: Contact your local or state environmental office for more information. Sources of BMP information include the state's environmental regulatory offices and state department of transportation offices.

• ACRONYMS •

This list includes acronyms commonly used in the construction industry, plus those encountered during interaction and correspondence with the regulatory community.

A&E	Architecture and Engineering
AAI	All Appropriate Inquiry
AASHTO	American Association of State Highway and Transportation
ACBM	Asbestos Containing Building Material
ACM	Asbestos Containing Material
ADEM	Alabama Department of Environmental Management
AHERA	Asbestos Hazard Emergency Response Act of 1986
AMD	Acrylamide Polymer
ANSI	American National Standards Institute
AOC	Administrative Orders on Consent
API	American Petroleum Institute
ASHRAE	American Society of Heating, Refrigerating and Air-Conditioning Engineers
ASME	American Society of Mechanical Engineers
AST	Above Ground Storage Tank
ASTM	American Society for Testing and Materials
ATSDR	Agency for Toxic Substances and Disease Registry
BACM	Best Available Control Measures
BACT	Best Available Control Technology
BAT	Best Available Treatment
BFM	Bonded Fiber Matrix
BMP	Best Management Practice
BOD	Biochemical Oxygen Demand
CAA	Compliance Assurance Agreement
CAS	Chemical Abstract System
CERCLA	Comprehensive Environmental Response, Compensation, and Liability Act
CERCLIS	Comprehensive Environmental Response, Compensation, and Liability Information System
CFCs	Chlorofluorocarbons
CFS	Cubic Feet Per Second
CG	Coast Guard

CHIPS	Chemical Hazard Information Profile System
CMP	Corrugated Metal Pipe
COC	Contaminants of Concern
COE	Corps of Engineers
CRM	Cultural Resources Manager
CWA	Clean Water Act
CZMA	Coastal Zone Management Act
DL	Detection Limit
DOJ	Department of Justice
DOL	Department of Labor
EA	Environmental Assessment
ECATTS	Environmental Compliance, Assessment, Training, and Tracking System
ECB	Erosion Control Blanket
EHS	Extremely Hazardous Substance
EIA	Environmental Impact Assessment
EIS	Environmental Impact Statement
ENF	Enforcement Action
EPA	Environmental Protection Agency
EPCA	Energy Policy and Conservation Act of 1975
EPCRA	Emergency Planning and Community Right-to-Know Act
EPSC	Erosion Prevention and Sedimentation Control
ERA	Ecological Risk Assessment
ERB	Engineering Review Board
ERT	Environmental Response Team
ESA	Endangered Species Act
ESHO	Environmental Safety and Health Officer
ESOH	Environmental, Safety, and Occupational Health
FACM	Friable Asbestos Containing Material
FAM	Friable Asbestos Material
FC	Fecal Coliform
FDA	US Food and Drug Administration
FFCA	Federal Facilities Compliance Act
FGM	Flexible Growth Matrix
FHA	Federal Housing Administration
FHWA	Federal Highway Administration
FRP	Facility Response Plan

FS	Forest Service
FUDS	Formerly Used Defense Sites
FWS	Fish and Wildlife Service
GWPD	Groundwater Protection Division
GWTP	Groundwater Treatment Plant
HABS	Historic American Building Survey
HAZWOPER	Hazardous Waste Operations and Emergency Response
HDPE	High Density Polyethylene
HSO	Health and Safety Officer
HTW	Hazardous and Toxic Waste
HW	Hazardous Waste
IAQ	Indoor Air Quality
ICS	Incident Command System
IW	Industrial Waste
IWTP	Industrial Waste Treatment Plant
LBP	Lead-Based Paint
LC	Lethal Concentration
LCA	Life Cycle Assessment
LD	Land Disposal
LEL	Lower Explosive Limit
LF	Landfill
LFL	Lower Flammability Limit
LFWA	Listing of Fish and Wildlife Advisories
LUC	Land Use Control
LUPZ	Land Use Planning Zone
MS4	Municipal Safety Data Sheets
MSW	Municipal Solid Waste
MSWLF	Municipal Solid Waste Landfill
NCP	National Oil and Hazardous Substances Contingency Plan (40 CFR 300)
NEPA	National Environmental Policy Act
NFS	National Forest Service
NHPA	National Historic Preservation Act
NORM	Naturally Occurring Radioactive Material
NOV	Notice of Violation
NPDES	National Pollutant Discharge Elimination System
NPL	National Priorities List

NRCS	Natural Resources Conservation Service
NRDA	Natural Resource Damage Assessment
NRHP	National Register of Historic Places
NRI	National Resources Inventory
NRM	Natural Resources Management
NSP	Nonpoint Source Pollution
NWR	National Wildlife Refuge
NWS	National Weather Service
ODS	Ozone Depleting Substance
OECA	US EPA Office of Enforcement and Compliance Assurance
OH&S	Occupational Health & Safety
OPA	Oil Pollution Act
OPA90	Oil Pollution Act of 1990
OSW	US EPA Office of Solid Waste
OUST	US EPA Office of Underground Storage Tanks
OWTS	On-site Wastewater Treatment System
P2	Pollution Prevention
PAM	Polyacrylamide or Polymer
PCBs	Polychlorinated Biphenyls
PCE or PERC	Tetrachloroethylene
PE	Professional Engineer
PHS	Public Health Service
PL	Public Law
PMT	Project Management Team
PST	Petroleum Storage Tank
PWS	Public Water System
QA	Quality Assurance
QA/QC	Quality Assurance/Quality Control
QAC	Quality Assurance Coordinator
QAM	Quality Assurance Manager
QAO	Quality Assurance Officer
QAPP	Quality Assurance Project Plan
QAS	Quality Assurance System
QAT	Quality Action Team
QCM	Quality Control Manager
QMP	Quality Management Plan

QCSM	Quality Control and Safety Manager
RA	Remedial Action
RA	Risk Analysis
RA	Risk Assessment
RAP	Remedial Action Plan
RCP	Reinforced Concrete Pipe
RCRA	Resource Conservation and Recovery Act
RCRIS	RCRA Information System
REC	Recognized Environmental Condition
ROD	Record of Decision
SARA	Superfund Amendment and Reauthorization Act
SCS	Soil Conservation Service
SDWA	Safe Drinking Water Act
SIP	State Implementation Plan
SME	Subject Matter Expert
SMP	Site Management Plan
SOP	Standard Operating Procedure
SPCC	Spill Prevention, Control, and Countermeasures
SQG	Small Quantity Generator
SW	Storm Water
SW	Surface Water
SWDA	Solid Waste Disposal Act
SWMA	Solid Waste Management Act
SWPPP	Storm Water Pollution Prevention Program
TMDL	Total Maximum Daily Load
TPH	Total Petroleum Hydrocarbons
TRM	Turf Reinforcement Mat
TS	Toxic Substances
TSCA	Toxic Substances Control Act
TSS	Total Suspended Solids
USACE	United States Army Corps of Engineers
USC	Unified Soil Classification
USDA	US Department of Agriculture
USEPA	US Environmental Protection Agency
USFS	US Forest Service
USFWS	US Fish and Wildlife Service

USGS	US Geological Survey
VFS	Vegetated Filter Strip
WQMP	Water Quality Management Plan
WQS	Water Quality Standards

Note: This list is not all inclusive. There are thousands of construction and compliance acronyms.